FEAR OF
FLY FISHING

Jack Ohman

A FIRESIDE BOOK
Published by Simon & Schuster
New York   London   Toronto   Sydney   Tokyo   Singapore

F

Fireside

Rockefeller Center
1230 Avenue of the Americas
New York, New York 10020

Published by the Simon & Schuster Trade Division

FIRESIDE and colophon are registered trademarks
of Simon & Schuster Inc.

Designed by Deirdre C. Amthor

Manufactured in the United States of America

10

Library of Congress Cataloging in Publication Data

Ohman, Jack.
Fear of fly fishing.

"A Fireside book."
1. Fly fishing—Humor.   2. Fly fishing—Caricatures and
cartoons.   3. American wit and humor, Pictorial.
I. Title.
PN6231.F62036   1988   741.5′973   88-18409

ISBN 0-671-66151-5

CONTENTS

ACKNOWLEDGMENTS

Writing and drawing about fly fishing is a heck of a lot harder than going fly fishing, but I'm glad I did this anyway. It made me realize just how many wonderful acquaintances I have made over the years by fishing with all sorts of stellar people. These are the people who helped me put this book together, even though none of the following had any idea what I was up to here.

I could probably write a whole book about fishing experiences with my dad; I'm sure most people could. By giving me a little Zebco rod and reel and taking me up to Three Lakes, near Marquette, Michigan, in the early '60s, he inadvertently started all this. Mark Strand is a great fisherman and even makes a living doing it. We lost and caught many fish together in Canada, Florida, Arkansas, Minnesota, and Wisconsin. In Oregon, Dick Thomas and I have won some and lost some, and there is also Bob Landauer, Phil Cogswell, Steve Carter, Brian Bell, Jack Hart, Dave Dunham, Jim Ramsey, and even my brother, Jim Ohman, who finally caught something the last time he was out here. Don and Peter Bundy are sorely missed by their fishing friends.

Herb Schaffner, who desperately wants to be a professional fisherman, bought *Fear of Fly Fishing* as a kind of out-of-Manhattan experience, but left for fame and fortune elsewhere. Still, thanks to him. I also thank Tim McGinnis of Fireside Books, who agreed to edit this book having fished only for perch with a worm.

My wife Jan edited *Fear of Fly Fishing*, but made no claims to understanding fly fishing other than its incredible drain on our finances. That's enough.

My agent Jeanne Hanson did the first retroactive book selling in publishing history. A gold watch and a laurel wreath to her for her usual good work.

FOR DAD

INTRODUCTION

An acquaintance of mine, a woman, was relating a harrowing tale of her father's, who was a senior member of a fly-fishing club. Her father, it seemed, had stopped attending the meetings because an unsavory element had infiltrated its ranks.

"What are we talking about here? Hell's Angels? Mimes? Carp fishermen?" I inquired.

"Yuppies," she replied. "They don't talk about fish in the meetings anymore. They talk about tune-ups on their Volvos and the benefits of bran and low-impact aerobics and Pinot Noirs. He said they occasionally talk about how expensive their equipment is."

Typical Y-worders. Or, more precisely:

Yuffies. Young Urban Fly-Fishermen.

Fly fishing used to be the exclusive province of 63-year-old men who had genetically attached Pork Pie hats. Things have changed in the '80s. There have been feature articles in *Esquire* and, for the love of God, *Gentlemen's Quarterly*, extolling the thrills and chills of fly fishing. There is even a TV commercial featuring a fly fisherman who is every inch the Yuffie. And, if there was any doubt left in your mind as to the current trendiness of the sport, *USA TODAY* has decreed that it's fashionable to be a fly fisherman, and devoted a front page story to the subject. Apparently a *USA TODAY* reporter saw somebody not matching the description of the prototypical fly fisherman standing in a stream and made a quick call back to Washington, DC (USA), to tell of his incredible Lifestyle Trend Discovery.

"Hi. National Desk please. Yeah, I just saw a 33-year-old lawyer in a fly-fishing get-up, and I think we can make a front-page out of it. How about 'WE'RE GETTING INTO FLIES MORE THAN EVER'?"

The next morning, it's on the front page, and every stressed-out, strung-out yuppie is reading the story. They all haul out their legal pads and write down all the key brand names, and when they get home, they call Orvis and L. L. Bean and Eddie Bauer and make their selections—swelling the nation's credit debt even further.

A couple of weeks later, all the Pork Pies who smell like the Fulton Fish Market after a refrigeration failure begin to notice all these smooth-jawed guys with no sideburns in the river dropping their rods and cracking the whip and splashing around in all the good pools. Naturally, they wonder just who these guys are with the inflatable vests and $400 boots.

I confirmed this trend last year while fishing for steelhead—unsuccessfully, as usual—in the North Umpqua River, just outside of Glide, Oregon. As I was pulling on my boots, a brand-new Chevy Blazer pulled up next to my car. On the side panels of the Blazer was the inscription, "San Francisco Fly Fishers." Out popped four guys with no sideburns and about $5,000 worth of equipment per San Francisco Fly Fisherperson. I didn't ask any questions, other than several that occurred to me silently as I wondered just what the heck a San Francisco Fly Fisher was.

Some questions are best left unasked.

They'll be gone as soon as *USA TODAY* spots the next Lifestyle Trend on which Yuppies can max out their MasterCards. But what we're really talking about in this book is fear, a primal fear, a fear of the unknown.

The fear of fly fishing.

Psychologists, when they're not taking our money, are always telling us to confront our fears. This is important, because there are millions of fishermen who fish for bass and sunfish and walleyes because they are afraid to pick up a fly rod. Of all pursuits mankind has devised to make you look stupid and uncoordinated, fly fishing is unquestionably number one. Here's why.

—A novice casting a 2/0 Woolly Worm can put you and others in direct physical danger.

—Fly equipment is so expensive that many think the Department of Defense has it contracted out.

—Fly fishing, with its arcane references to WF-6-F lines and 9 ft. 6 weight rods and CFO IV reels with Multipliers, rivals Boolean algebra and quantum mechanics in complexity.

—There are so many permutations of flies available that choosing one sends most people back to the decision, "Do I use the entire worm or do I cut it in two?"

Let's confront our fears. Let's conquer the fear of fly fishing.

Gearing Up

Sparing the Rod

A fly fisherman's first rod should be modest. No one should start out with an Orvis split bamboo or a Winston, even if their credit line goes along with it. A first rod should weigh the far side of a pound, be constructed of industrial electrical conduit, be as flexible as a telephone pole, and have the guides look as if they were wrapped by Helen Keller. Only then will you appreciate a good rod.

The first rod can be purchased at a hardware store. You'll find them in a plastic garbage can next to the Day-Glo bobber display. A really tony first rod should run about $20. Make sure it has a fairly obscure name brand, such as "Cast-O-Rama" or "Fish'n'Buddy." The rod should be about as flexible as a 36-ounce Louisville Slugger;

you'll also want to select a model with a defective reel seat, providing you with the unparalleled thrill of reeling in a big trout while holding the reel in your hand, instead of having it securely attached to your rod.

After you've fished with the First Rod for a couple of trips, you'll need a pretext to get rid of it. "Accidentally" closing the trunk of your car on the tip, "dropping" it in a raging torrent, or just "forgetting" it at a pool are all acceptable excuses to go out and blow a lot of dough for a new one. After you've ditched your starter rod, you'll need a new one. Before Orvis gets your MasterCard number, let's review the different types of rods:

Long Rods Who doesn't want a long rod? If you live west of Minneapolis, these things are an absolute must. A nine-and-a-half footer will sling your weight-forward line halfway to Omaha if you've got even the slightest tailwind, but they can also wrap eighty feet of Cortland around your neck and dig a Muddler Minnow into your temple laughing all the way. There are salmon rods up to 14 feet long, but you're casting to fish, not Buicks.

However, on Eastern streams you'll be regarded as somewhat of a vulgarian; you might as well show up on the Neversink with a Snoopy Zebco and a loaf of Wonder Bread. In the Midwest, you'll be regarded as a pretentious exhibitionist with money to throw into the stream. A straw cowboy hat complements the long rod and telegraphs the signal to fellow fishermen that you're from A Big Western State and you catch Big Western Fish.

Short Rods They're a novelty item, a conversation starter: "What is that thing, a car antenna?" Most trout go on to their reward before you can land them, due to the extreme care you have to use in order not to break the spider web diameter leader. They're a real hoot for fishing with midges in a narrow stream, but you can only land a nine-inch brookie in slack water before the whole affair is jerked out of your hands. Those who live by the two weight die by the two weight; catching neon tetra-sized trout is fine, but the minute a Large Specimen snaps your one-pound leader you'll be back to a six weight and barbed hooks, and need a NASA recovery team standing by.

Cane Rods They're strictly for dry fishing. Fishing with them is Art, but who wants to fish with something they're afraid to touch? Fishing with a cane rod is like playing rugby in your grandmother's sitting room; the delicacy with which you have to pursue the sport is usually not worth the hassle. I sometimes have the sensation that I'm posing for an oil painting when I've used one. Graphite has the edge on durability, but proponents may argue that Babe Ruth would not use an aluminum bat. When you're trying to jerk that two-buck fly out of the bushes across the stream, you may want something that doesn't seem to make little whimpering noises when you haul back on it.

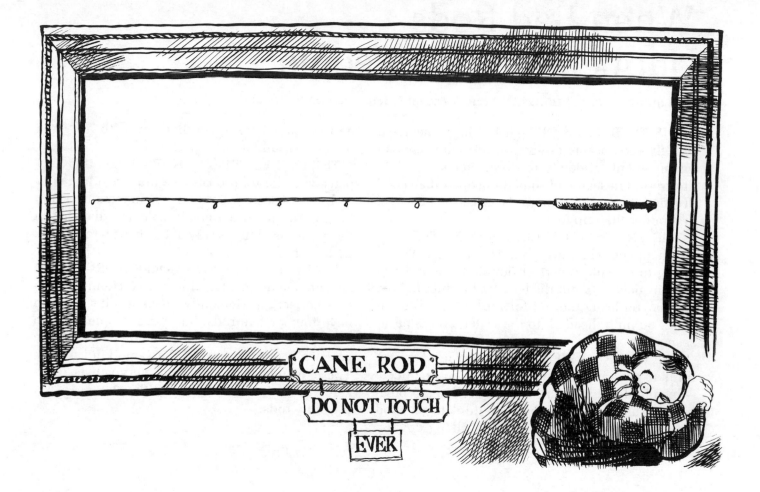

When Bad Rods Happen to Good People

Here are some of the things that always seem to happen with fly rods:

THE TIP BREAKS OFF—It has been theorized that fly rods act as dowsing sticks and have an inconvenient tendency to drive themselves into the ground in search of something other than good dry fly water. The remedy is to carry them reel first rather than tip first.

THE END SECTION COMES OFF—This usually happens when everyone is watching. You're trying to execute a perfect double-haul, and you have neglected to put the ferrules together tightly, and as you bring the rod forward, it comes off at about 80 mph, heads into the water, and is never seen again.

THE ROD AS A WEAPON—It's easier than you think to get whipped in the face—it doesn't tickle —by a buddy's rod while you're walking through heavy brush. It's easier than you think to get a rod tip in your mouth when you're walking down a narrow path behind another guy with a fly rod who stops suddenly.

THE GUIDES FREEZE OVER—When this happens, you should probably be indoors oiling your reel, but most fly fishermen are monomaniacs and hence are out in extremely cold weather. Ice in the guides is nature's way of telling you to go back to the car.

YOU BECOME A ROD COLLECTOR—This is an untreatable mental illness, like Hummel figurine collecting. Generally speaking, it's okay to have four or five rods, but some people have to have every single one that is manufactured every year, or worse, several of the same kind of rod. These people become fly-rod survivalists, hunkered down in their bunkers with a 200-year supply of fly rods.

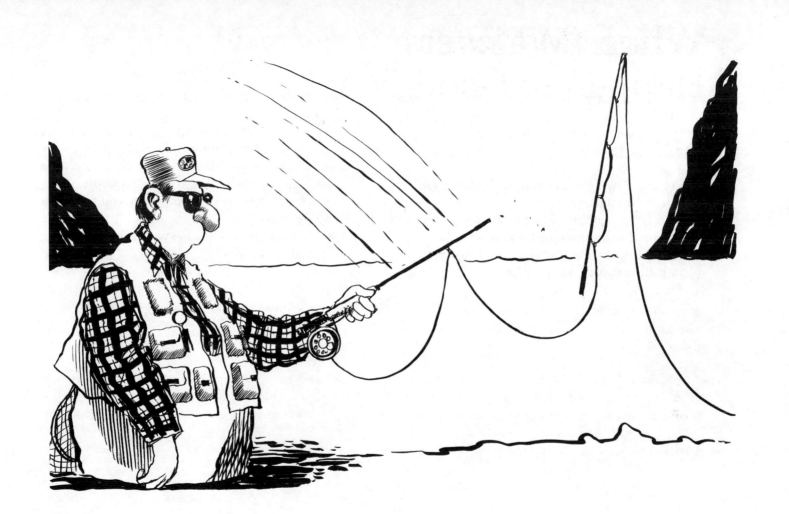

Weight Watchers

Rods and lines are rated by "weight," like motor oil and how you look in a swimming suit. Here is a handy table to help you determine what weight rod and line to use:

—11 ft., 8 weight—Salmon, Yankee Class nuclear submarines

—9½ ft., 7 weight—Steelhead, large tires, submerged fishermen under 200 pounds

—9 ft., 6 weight—Browns you'll never land in a million years, smaller tires

—8 ft., 5 weight—Normal-sized trout, boots, your lost six-pack

—7½ ft., 4 weight—Stunted trout, anemic brookies, chubs, branches

—7 ft., 3 weight—May get your fly and leader back to you, assuming there's no wind

—6½ ft., 2 weight—Breaks when you talk over 60 decibels

—6 ft., 1 weight—Breaks if you think the wrong thoughts about it

Reel Life

Two schools of thought dominate the selection of a reel. School A—the disposable-income school—says that skimping on a reel is next to folly, that a good reel is indispensable for wrestling in the lunkers and keeping your line in decent repair.

School B—the thrifty school—points out that a fly reel is a glorified line storage compartment with no true utility, like a spinning reel. The line just sits there until you strip it out, and then you usually end up stripping the line back in when you're landing a fish. So what's the point? The point is that a big fish will leave you standing there with a handful of greasy screws, nuts and springs as you bid adieu to your fish, line, leader, and fly.

When you are landing a fish, you will note that very little reeling is actually done; the line is always wound up around your hand in coils—or incomprehensible curlicues within the reel itself while a fish is pushing the outside of the drag specifications. Little rivulets of sweat trickle down your brow as you attempt to untangle the mess inside your reel, and just as you're about to haul out the knife and cut the snarl apart, the fish spares you the trouble.

The appearance of a fly reel is thankfully different from the latest fad in spinning-reel design, which is to make the reel look like a 35mm Nikon camera. On new spinning reels, you'll find all sorts of numerical charts regarding line weights and spool capacities, switches and levers—everything but a lens. Fly reels all basically look the same—like they could double as kitchen-drain covers.

Unreel Things

The easiest way to mark yourself as a total and complete rube is to fall for the siren song of the automatic reel. They are only socially acceptable if you have one arm. They are especially constructed to go on the end of a $14-dollar rod and pull in sunnies and crappies, which frequently find themselves chewing on the rod tip about three-tenths of a second after inhaling the fly.

Complete wimps purchase "reel mitts," which are a kind of sleeping bag for reels. Banging your reel on the rocks gives it character; it shows you go fishing all the time, and a reel mitt makes you look like a candy-ass who's afraid to get fish slime on your hands.

Hell on Reels

What are some of the things that can go wrong with a reel while you're fishing?

THEY FALL OFF THE REEL SEAT—Invariably occurs when you're trying to land a 21-inch rainbow. Some rods have a disconcerting design flaw that magically unscrews the reel-seat nuts just when the fish is making a final run.

THE LEADER BECOMES ENMESHED IN THE GEARS—This isn't as bad as when it happens on a closed-face reel (when that happens you should throw it into the water for the fish to get a good laugh, because you'll never be able to repair it). It always happens 30 minutes before sunset, when the trout are taking the hatch like piranhas would take Elsie the Borden Cow.

THE LINE IS TIED INTO A KING-HELL KNOT—This happens as a big honker is making a desperate run, the reel is screaming bloody murder, you're thinking you're going to get your picture in the newspaper if you ever land the sucker, and suddenly: The Big Knot. A nanosecond later, you're standing there with limp line and the task of taking 45 minutes to untie the Gordian Knot.

THE SPOOL WON'T CLICK IN—It happens on less expensive, more complicated reels, and there doesn't seem to be any rational explanation, but the bugger just won't snap on. A claw hammer applied at the point of distress may get you back in business.

Getting the Boot

There are two types of boots: those that permit the frigid waters of the stream to course through your toes, and those that do not. Leakage is a constant battle, and in warmer climates some fly fishermen just say the hell with it and wade without benefit of protection. This may present a problem when it's 38 degrees and you're breaking chunks of ice off your line guides.

Hip boots are preferred if you're in a dribble of a stream and you have to do a lot of walking. Chest waders, particularly the insulated rubber jobs, make you feel like Neil Armstrong and are difficult to remove should a Bladder Emergency arise.

However, the prime advantage of hip boots is that stepping off into a hole and slipping off a shelf won't require anglers with a better sense of balance to fish you out. That's embarrassing, but it's even more embarrassing to be seen floating upside down, trapped in your Goodyear Blimp-like chest waders.

The disadvantage of hip boots is that they limit your wading to the point where you might actually have to learn how to cast properly. Getting into cold waders in the morning is like trying to forcibly dress a seal in a spandex leotard. It isn't natural, and it's frustrating when you're doing it, but it's great fun to watch somebody else squirming on the ground, legs skyward, and syntax peppered with nasty Anglo-Saxon interjections.

There are the neoprene-leather boot waders, but they're almost too cute for words, and they make fishermen look like they've been dipped in chocolate. Fly-weight chest waders are great, but you have to wear old tennis shoes over them, and, frankly, you'll look like an escapee from a state mental hospital.

Vested Interests

Vests should be mobile versions of your car glove compartment—jammed to the seams with useless trash that may come in handy in an emergency, like the AAA Guide to Iowa Theme Parks.

A short vest has a tendency to make you feel like you're wearing a bra stuffed with newspapers if you've packed it improperly. Most pockets on a short vest can only accommodate a first-class stamp-sized box with a couple of size 20 cream midges. The two front pockets should be big enough to accommodate two ice chests, with enough room left over to park a '66 Dodge Dart.

On the exterior of the vest should be a pair of nail nippers capable of cutting your index finger off at the first knuckle. Don't try this at home. You will also note a piece of shearling sheepskin or two on the outside of the vest, which is a kind of scrapyard for junked flies—the broken barb, the loose tinsel, the missing wing, the unraveled head that you're really going to get around to fixing someday—that have sentimental value. In the summer, you will learn the painful truth about owning the dark green-colored vest: it's like wearing a solar panel.

Inflatable vests are a good idea if you're fishing in the Ganges, but they sometimes have a disconcerting tendency to go off at inopportune moments. Avoid surprise embraces.

Playing It Close to the Vest

Here's what you should expect to find in the average fly vest:

—134 flies (128 with hook points corroded off because you were too lazy to dry them off).

—16 4/0 streamers that you bought because you were just starting fly fishing, and didn't know what you were doing.

—23 empty leader packages.

—1 leader package with an actual leader in it.

—Hershey bar (with almonds) from 1969—just in case.

—Replacement hook file to replace the other six dozen hook files you accidentally dropped in the stream.

—Nipper reel with no nippers on the end.

—Nipper reel with nippers on the end.

—Boot patch repair kit with hole in the cement tube.

—Hand vise you whimsically ordered and will never use.

—Big green Glad Bag in the hope that you'll need it for a 37-pound Brown.

—Salmon eggs in plain brown wrapper.

Net Work

Nets are very awkward to carry around while you're trout fishing. They always seem to get caught on a branch as you're walking along—you keep moving forward, the elastic stretches to its maximum tensile strength, and then the net breaks off and hits you directly between the shoulder blades at about 2,000 feet per second.

Shoddy nets will weigh about ten pounds and appear to have been tennis racquets in a previous incarnation. They will have netting that seems to engulf trout and consume them. Good nets can be inexpensive and still avoid acting as Cuisinarts. Highbrows like the burnished lacquered wood, but you may hesitate about dipping your precious myrtlewood baby in the water, which kind of defeats the whole purpose of the device.

To net a trout, chase it wildly in the stream until you have scared it to death, or chase it up onto the bank and throw the net over it.

Trout Fishing in America

The Trout Fishing Technocracy

Sometime in the evolution of the sport of fly fishing—I place the exact date at July 20, 1969, the day men landed on the moon—fly fishing became inexplicably arcane and loaded with technological jargon.

Fly fishermen can be divided into two broad groups: those who don't really know what an 800 grain WF-6-S is, and those who do. The those-who-do group are the fly-fishing technocrats.

Fly-fishing technocrats have to make everything complicated. You can't just say to a fly-fishing technocrat, "Tie on a brown nymph, will ya?" You have to say, "Manually implement an Ephemeroptera paradigm, will ya?" They know every Latin name of every bug—they hate it when you call a fly a "bug"—and give you a look like you didn't prep at the right school if you refer to your rod as a pole.

They also know that a 7X leader tippet is .004 inches in diameter, how many feet per second the river is flowing, and what the pH level in the water is. They own LED digital landing nets. Listening to the fly-fishing technocrat talk about fishing is about like listening to Mission Control: "Yeah, I got an anomaly in my 6X so I'm retying a 5X and putting a terrestrial on."

Roger. Copy, over and out.

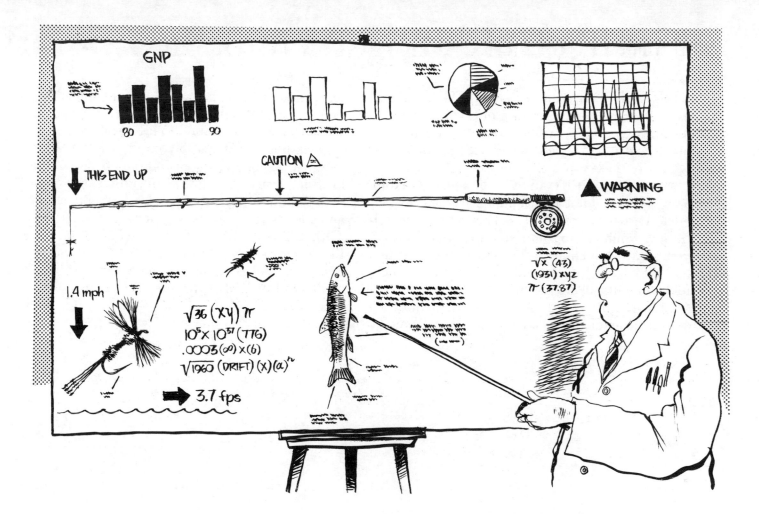

Fishing Guides

If you have never been fly fishing before, you may wish to employ the services of a guide. This almost always takes on the elements of a particularly nasty blind date, so caveat emptor, and watch for these types of guides:

AM DISC JOCKEY TYPE—He never shuts up. You're trying to at least enjoy a pastoral experience, and he's constantly jabbering at you, critiquing your casting and standing right next to you chewing bubble gum, Red Man, a Slim Jim, and a Swisher Sweet. And he always calls you a nickname like "Pal" or "Bud."

STRONG SILENT TYPE—The evil twin of the above. He barely utters a word, only to tell you it's time to move to the next pool, offering no advice, suggestions, fly patterns, or bawdy rejoinders.

SCIENTIFIC ANGLER TYPE—Makes you sit through hours of incredibly boring lectures about the life cycle of Plecoptera and the physics of line loading. Usually a Ph.D. in Philosophy who dropped out of the rat race. Thinks you're stupid and spends your money on dope.

KINDERGARTEN TEACHER TYPE—Treats you like a five-year-old. Says "very good" after every cast and makes embarrassingly obvious statements with the same vocal quality as Mr. Rogers. "Can you say, 'nymph'? I knew you could," and "That's Mr. Reel at the end of Mr. Rod."

Getting into the Mainstream

This isn't as easy as it looks. Neophytes will bound willy-nilly into rapids and have their bodies recovered three months later. Seasoned pros will inch gingerly into the stream, wearing felt soles and stream cleats big enough to take out a major-league second baseman, and then bound into the rapids, slipping on the nearest available slimy rock and land ass-over-teacups, coming up for air 60 yards downstream.

Positioning Yourself

Find a likely-looking stretch of water. A likely-looking stretch of water will have trout jumping and taking flies that resemble nothing that you have in your fly box. After you have gotten yourself out of the water after falling ass-over-teacups, head 60 yards back upstream and get in again, don't jump in like you were invited into a hot tub by Daryl Hannah.

Find a big rock underwater and wedge your toes under it, kicking up sediment and scaring away any trout within a three-county radius. Stand very still until the trout start jumping. While you are standing there, try to remember all the entomology you have learned in serious trout-fishing books. After deciding that you couldn't tell an emerging blue dun mayfly from a U-boat, look in your fly box and tie on a fly.

Matching the Hatch

Look down at the water. Reach under a rock and see if there are any caddis houses (tiny shells that the caddis insects emerge from when they hatch). If you find one, make clucking noises to yourself about how scientific you are about all this, that the trout have no chance of survival, and then tie on a Royal Coachman. Trout have vastly overrated powers of observation. The proper fly should be one that cost more than two bucks. Failing that, look for a fly that doesn't have the eyelet rusted over or a big glob of head cement on it. If it matches the hatch, great. If it doesn't, well, it's not like wearing brown shoes with a blue suit.

Making Your Presentation

Having tied on the Royal Coachman, your next task is to put the fly close enough to the trout so that its sophisticated "lateral line" can sense its presence and then reject it. Watch the rises. A rise is a trout's way of laughing at you. Having selected the rising fish you want to cast to, strip out your line. The trout will then move about six feet farther away than your line will travel. You are now ready to make your presentation; or, in layman's terms, "cast" to the trout.

Psyching Out the Trout

Okay. You've been floating the dry fly over the trout's nose for 45 minutes. It's time to go to plan B. Apply psychology: Be the Trout. What does a trout want? A mouth full of feathers, fur, and piano wire? Negative; he wants juicy insects, and if he can't have that, he's not looking for artistic quality in your casting.

The best way to catch a trout on a dry fly is time-tested: Stop paying attention. Pull out a six-pack from one of your vest pockets, imitate the background vocals of the Ronettes' greatest hits, do anything but pay attention. Cast absently, slovenly, incompetently. Get out of the water and drag the fly along the edge of the bank while thinking about how you would ask Diane Sawyer out to dinner. Trout hate not being the center of attention. Once you've pissed the trout off, he's ready to strike.

The Strike

Wham. He's on, and you're in the alpha brain-wave state. Wake up, take up the 80 feet of slack line that is inevitably there when you get a strike, and plot your strategy. One thing to bear in mind is the trout is probably slightly more surprised than you are; you don't have an unanticipated hook in your jaw—he does. There is the tendency to reel until the gears melt and get the fish in, but remember, this is recreation, not an Olympic trial. Speed isn't a factor. Let the trout do what it's going to do. You can't negotiate with terrorists.

The Trout's Strategy, Such As It Is

The trout is looking for serrated edges. He's looking for a branch, a sharp rock you could perform brain surgery with, anything he can find to hack the two-pound leader in half and leave you heading back to the fly store. If he can't cut your leader, he'll want to tie it to something. He wants to make your leader an Alexander Calder mobile and, above all, he wants to make you look bad. Notice that trout never seem to hook themselves over nice, obstructionless sandy shoals; notice that it always happens over the piscatorial equivalent of the South Bronx.

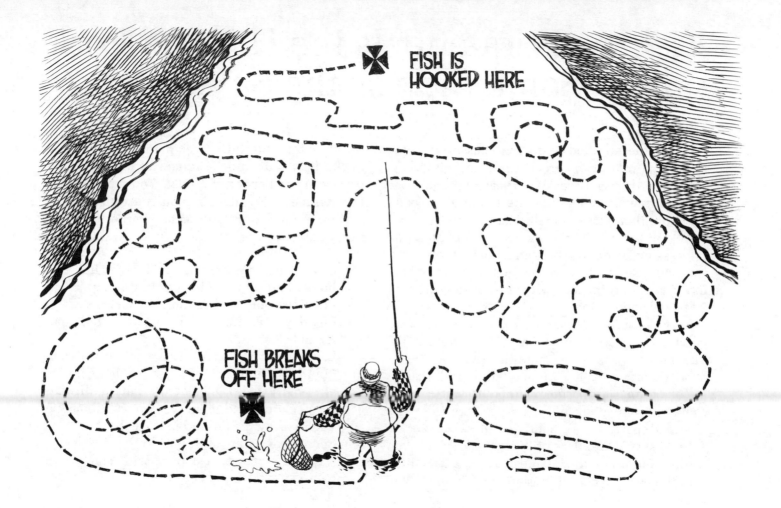

Fishing Etiquette: Is the Henry's Fork on the Same Side as the Salad Fork?

With all the huddled fly-fishing masses yearning to breathe free in the great American wilderness alongside thousands of other yearning, huddling fly fishermen, fishing etiquette is rapidly becoming more than just a social nicety. Like the inevitable loudmouth in the movie theater doing an impression of both Siskel and Ebert, there is always going to be the dweeb who throws Frito bags in the river, or the boor who crashes into the drift 20 feet ahead of you.

In the East, where you are likely to be pelvis to pelvis with people who have run amok in the Manhattan Orvis shop, there has to be some sort of social order, even if Manhattan doesn't place a lot of emphasis on social order. If you commit some gross misdemeanor in an Eastern river, the offended party is probably either a lawyer or knows several underemployed ones, and you could wind up on the business end of a lawsuit.

In the West, where things are less litigious, you could be the unfortunate recipient of a haymaker in the Polaroids and be forced to navigate your river without benefit of a boat. You may wish to observe the following common courtesies on the stream, or maybe not. But be forewarned: You are likely to be drowned if you:

—Say, "I see you're catching a lot of fish in this hole. Shouldn't you be toddling along?"
—Practice your backcast on New Jersey's opening day and impale the nostril of a man named Cheech.
—Launch an 18-foot bass boat christened "Lunker Plunker" in reflective letters in a glassy dry fly stretch of the Battenkill, and then claim, indignantly, the maribou jig you're throwing around is a dry fly.
—Encourage your children to hold a rock-skipping contest in a pool with eight guys fishing the tailwaters.

—Thrash out into the rapids, screaming, "Hey! Can somebody tie my fly on for me?"

—Say, "Excuse me. Is my ghetto blaster going to bother you?"

—Throw 30,000 carp fingerlings into the stream, announcing, "These fish are a delicacy in Asia."

Central Casting

When you're first starting out in fly fishing, your friends will give you a lot of brave talk about how easy it is to fly cast. While it appears, to the novice, that it is as easy as learning how to use a buggy whip, this is precisely the effect that you will be trying to avoid.

As you begin fly casting, you will probably note a satisfying "crack" as you bring the line forward. This is the buggy-whip effect, and other fly fishermen on the stream will begin laughing to themselves or right out loud, depending on how rigorously streamside etiquette is observed. You may also notice that you will probably end up with a good 40 or 50 feet of line coiled neatly in front of you, which is the embarrassing accompanying sight gag that goes hand in hand with the buggy-whip noise. After a few days—or perhaps years—of not being able to cast more than ten feet in any direction, you will probably want to learn how to do it right.

Getting a Grip On

There are three ways to hold the rod. The first is a handshake grip, the second is a modified handshake with an extended thumb, and the third is more of the same, except with an extended forefinger. If you can't even get one of these three right, you are probably doomed to bank fishing for carp with doughballs.

Rod Warrior

Bring the rod briskly up to 12 o'clock—no need to adjust for a different time zone—and strip out ten feet of line. Begin waving the rod around like a whip fetishist until you have stripped out another 20 feet. Pick up the coiled line in your left hand and start flagellating the water until a frothy meringue forms on the water in front of you. Maybe the fish will hide underneath it and you can toss a stick of dynamite into the foam.

Giving Them a Line

Disregard the above. Bring the rod up to 12 o'clock and gently but firmly bring the rod forward until you've stripped out enough line. As you bring the line back, you will feel tension. This is called "loading," or you have hooked an inconveniently located branch behind you. This is called "snagging." If you're not snagged, at the precise instant you feel the line loading, keep tension on the line as you bring it forward and let the line slip through your fingers. The line should then pass rapidly through the guides and put the fly in the precise location you wanted it, if you haven't snagged the fly on a protrusion—your ear, say.

A Cast of Thousands

THE ROLL CAST

This type of cast is to be performed if you have a brushy bank or otherwise limited space. Strip out 20 feet of line and bring the rod tip up to vertical. Snap the tip down suddenly and watch the line do a gentle roll toward your target. Note: Trout are not impressed by your casting ability, so don't expect a gratuitous strike.

THE SLINGSHOT CAST

Purchase a Wrist Rocket or other type of slingshot. Put the fly in the leather thong—3/0 size hook or larger—and pull back on the sling. Release.

THE S-CAST

To perform an S-Cast, jerk up on the rod tip and wiggle it around until you form the letter "S" with the line. Real easy.

THE BOW-AND-ARROW CAST

Take a 60-pound compound bow and tie your leader on to a metal arrow. Pull back. Make sure you have plenty of backing and that your buddy isn't standing in front of you. If he is, put an apple on his head to divert the arrow's flight path. Effective in shallow water where you can see the fish. Aim for the trout's head. Release.

THE DOUBLE HAUL

A long-distance cast. Grasp the rod firmly in your right hand and haul back. Throw entire rig into stream after completely giving up all hope of ever learning how to cast.

Fly Tying: Money-saver or Mania?

People who can barely lace up their wing-tips suddenly think they can tie flies. New fly tiers have interesting motivations for taking up this hobby: They can save money on flies, or they think it's relaxing. Not likely; it is easier to relax performing neurological laser surgery, and only in fly tying would you pay 40 bucks for the neck of a dead chicken. But if you are really intent on tying flies, here are some pointers.

Do not buy a so-called Fly-Tying Kit, particularly if it costs ten bucks and was assembled in Seoul. In those kits are included:

—A vise made of an unidentifiable alloy barely capable of holding a 6/0 gang hook.
—50 yards of orange chenille.
—Crazy Glue.
—Maribou feathers in colors not normally associated with anything between Infrared and Ultraviolet.
—Shark hooks.
—Christmas tree tinsel.
—Shocking pink wet fly cape.

—Instructions in Korean and English as translated by Korean grade-school dropouts:

"Hook, goodly set in mandible of vise object thing. Appropriate down from poultry into hand? Yes. Knotting thread into hook will please. To be additional, orange chenille, shocking Pink feather, Green Maribou plumage is nice. On hook, to put. Tying more and more to taste, finish. Crazy Glue is applying all over, tinsel is like wrapping so very finely as to impersonate water bugs? Yes."

No.

Okay. You've persisted this far. You must really want to do this. This is a zero-sum pursuit. You have been warned.

First of all, you'll need a vise. There are essentially three types of vises:

—The Thompson A vise. This type of vise can hold hooks so small that—well, put it this way: You'll never be able to tie a size-28 hair wing Adams, so don't worry about it.

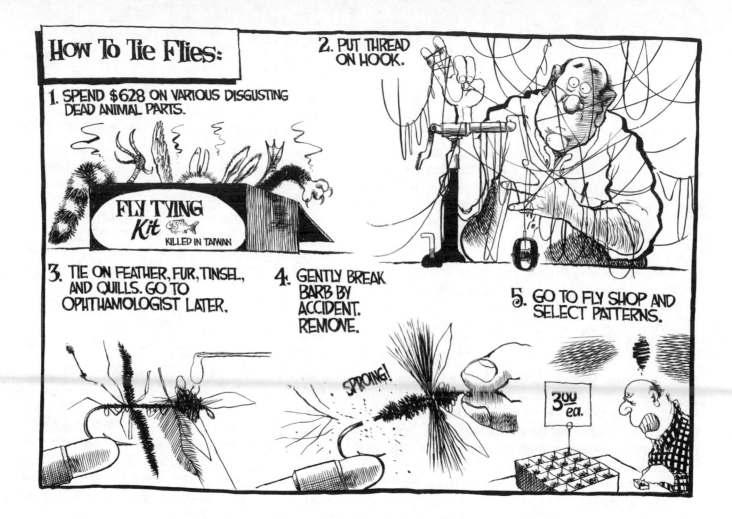

—The Thompson B vise, which is the cut-rate version of the A vise. Instead of the A vise clamping lever, the B vise has a screw-in handle that tightens the jaws. It is mud ugly.
—The Rotating vise, which is used by professional fly-tiers and gives you a 360-degree view of your fly. You'll just end up getting feathers and head cement and other assorted fly-tying goo all over your lap.

Now we're getting to the point where you have to use your stubby little fingers. Practice tying your shoes a couple of times. Write your name so that all the letters are legible. Crack your knuckles. You'll need the following tools now that you're all limber.

—A pair of scissors.
—A kind of a weird metal dealie.
—A long thing with a loop on the end.
—A kind of pencil-like job with a hole in it.
—A pretzel type of a thing that is virtually incomprehensible.

As the Fur Flies

There are a lot of fly patterns—none officially recognized or sanctioned—that you can tie with stuff just lying around your home, particularly if you live in a barnyard or the woods. For these, you can improvise fly-tying material with a minimum of fuss.

Own any cats? Hate them? Pulling out generous tufts of fur gives you lots of nice gray dubbing material and keeps Tabby on his toes. Do you have a dog? God knows there's enough dog hair just lying around the house, so you don't even have to appropriate it from Fido while he's still using it. A collie's fur makes excellent hair-wing streamers. Go to a petting zoo and ask to see the peacocks. When the gendarmes aren't looking, borrow some plumage. I personally have deer tails dating back to the mid-'70s from when guilty suburban hunters dropped them off with my dad.

Tying One On

Put your hook in the vise. If it's smaller than a size 12, consult your ophthalmologist beforehand. Now wind on the incredibly fine thread all up and down the shank of the hook. After you've accidentally broken the incredibly fine thread, start over.

You are now ready to tie on the tail. Take a hackle feather, tear off about 15 hackle points, and tie them on. Make sure the tail is sticking straight out. Having performed this procedure, get out some dubbing wax and rub a little gob of it between your thumb and forefinger. Warning: It's pretty gross. Now get some rabbit fur or some of that synthetic stuff gleaned from carpet remnants and kind of wrap it around the thread that should be hanging down. It isn't? Hmm.

Anyway, you are now ready to tie on the wings. This is a real pain, particularly if you're trying to tie on duck feathers. You have to make them stand up just so, and one always seems to wind up on the bottom of the hook. Keep the glue off it. Oops. Nice move.

Now that you've welded the wings together, it's time to tie on the hackle. Tie the hackle feather just ahead of the welded wings, and then wrap it around the shank of the hook. Take the end of the feather and tie it off. The artistic part comes into play here. Tie off the head. Put a blob of black glue on it. Make sure you don't put it over the eyelet. Whoopsie daisy. Too late. Now take the hook out of the vise. You'll want to avoid breaking the barb off the hook. I said, you wanted to avoid breaking the barb off the hook. Gee. You'll have to start all over again.

Trout: Do They Exist?

Sometimes fly fishing for trout can be a kind of ontological exercise. You cast until your rotator cuff cries out for clemency, and the stream appears biologically dead. You find yourself questioning why you are standing in a river at 6:34 A.M.—temperature a crisp 33 degrees—water leaking slowly but steadily into your right boot, breaking ice out of your line guides. Then you start questioning the very existence of trout.

Of course, you have seen pictures of trout in *Fly Fisherman* and *Outdoor Life*. But they can do some pretty amazing things with photography these days, and you wonder whether the so-called trout are really sculptures or maybe just suckers spray-painted silver, while the photographer has his lens set on a soft-fuzz setting. You wonder whether or not you are the victim of some grand hoax perpetrated by the Trilateral Commission to keep the middle class at bay. For academic purposes, let's make the assumption that trout do exist, and that a mere mortal can actually catch them.

Rainbow Trout *Salmo hatcheri*

The rainbow trout is probably the most frequently caught trout species, due to a silly theory called "put and take." Put and take is the practice of dumping zillions of seven-inch rainbows into a stream, and then permitting a like number of meat fishermen to catch them and take them home to rot in their refrigerators. Unfortunately, these little hatchery fish are so dumb that they can't reproduce and thus every year must be replaced by more dumb hatchery fish. The logic is along the lines of, "We had to destroy the village in order to save it."

On a more aesthetic plane, rainbows are arguably the most beautiful of the trout, and have perfected leader breaking and jumping—"air time"—to the extent that other trout seem to be on Valium by comparison. Steelhead run about six to 20 pounds, and are like UFOs: They're always sighted and caught by people you wouldn't normally define as credible. Winter steelheading with flies is only for severe claustrophobia cases and masochists who are trying to keep their arms limbered up for opening day.

Brown Trout *Salmo lethargii*

Introduced in 1885 from Germany, the brown trout is the most adaptable trout, and reproduces easily. It also grows to sizes that will take off all of your new 30-buck double-taper fly line, your one hundred yards of cotton line backing, your hand-tied leader, and your meticulously tied Dark Hendrickson and weave intricate patterns in the submerged branches and rocks before spitting it out.

Brown trout are—surprise—mostly brown. Big ones are very dark, and have huge underslung jaws like bulldogs. They have the reputation for wallowing around on the bottom and not jumping often enough. Brown trout—particularly ones that graze like cattle on the bottoms of reservoirs—are not exactly aerobically fit. A brown trout could get a recliner and ESPN and a Schmidt Sport Pack and be perfectly content. But try landing a large one sometime; they shake their heads like pit bulls and then become sheer dead weight, testing your tackle to the point where you feel like you're trying to reel in a Volkswagen.

Golden Trout *Salmo nonexistus*

The golden trout is an alleged species that is said to live in the High Sierras, probably in the same mountain range as Bigfoot. The only known footage of a golden trout is an eight-second film taken in 1965, and it's pretty grainy.

Brook Trout *Salmo minisculus*

Brook trout run about two-and-a-quarter inches, on the national average. If you deliberately set out to catch brookies, you are in for a lot of guilt feelings about maiming the little buggers, because they are small. Oh, once in a while you'll tie into a big one, say seven or eight inches long, but you'll need to use live bait and Ford Fenders for one of those.

Brook trout are technically char, but nobody seems to know why they're not called brook char. Not as appetizing, more than likely. "Pass me some of that delicious brook char." Preblackened fish. Brook trout have beautiful purple, pink, and yellow spots on their sides, as if you're just waking up and looking at them after an all-night bender.

Actual size

Cutthroat Trout *Salmo inaccessablis*

Most of the good fishing for cutthroats happened about a hundred years ago, so you're not likely to catch many, unless you are willing to trek many miles, past the simple graves of all the unfit fat guys who tried the same thing. If you climb high into mountains, they are present, but they are about the size of a sperm cell.

Cutthroat are similar in appearance to rainbows, but they have a little slash under their jaw, which is what you may feel like doing after trying to catch them. In reservoirs, they're easier to catch, and they grow to immense size, but you may have to use the ultimate fishing contradiction in terms: a "fly-rod flatfish."

Cutthroats are sometimes known as "natives," which means that they have been caught by all the natives who live nearby.

Flies in the Soup

Fly the Friendly Dries

Dry-fly fishing is a lot trickier than fishing wet flies. Wet flies are the worms of fly fishing; it frankly doesn't require a heck of a lot of finesse to catch a trout on a wet, and you might as well hook on a bobber. The dry fly has to land precisely right, gently simulating the landing of the mayfly. Think of your fly as a tiny helicopter cutting its engines to surprise the lurking Vietcong trout, but forget how Vietnam turned out. Some dry-fly hints:

—Don't try to jerk a dry fly out of your earlobe. Gently remove it with the forceps hanging from your vest.
—Don't say, "Here, fishy, fishy, fishy."
—Don't surreptitiously put a Lime Gummi Bear on the fly; it hinders flotation and trout don't seem to like that flavor.
—Although it has a slightly intoxicating aroma, do not drink your dry-fly flotant as an alcohol substitute.
—There is no credible physical or photographic evidence to suggest that anyone has ever successfully tied on a dry fly smaller than size 16.
—Dry-fly hooks turn to lead when a hatch starts.
—Dry flies only seem to float properly when you've accidentally spilled your fly box into the stream.

The Dry Fly

The dry fly operates on the as-yet-unproven principle that a piece of metal can float on the surface of the water. Archimedes tried it and was only able to work out the theory of displacement, and most fly fishermen who don't hook their dry fly onto a piece of Styrofoam reaffirm that time-honored principle.

The theory is that the dry fly imitates a floating mayfly, and trout actually come up and grab it. Okay, it happens. But mostly, dry flies spend most of their time wet. Various chemical outfits have peddled fly flotants, which are about as buoyant as the airplane seats doubling as life preservers. Good luck.

TRUE DRY FLIES

Styrofoam Quill

Bobber Coachman

Cork Cream

The Wet Fly

This group of flies imitates mayflies as they are about to come to the surface, as well as drowned terrestrials. They are also the easiest to tie. After you've experienced the exquisite agony of trying to make the hair wing stand up on a Royal Wulff, you will understand and thrill to the ease of tying a White Miller or a Leadwing Coachman.

Wet flies are also easier to fish with. You don't need to have the trout grade your casts on a ten-point scale as you sense is the case when you cast a dry fly. You can be sloppy, inept, clumsy (in short, human) when you fish with wet flies. They're more relaxing.

TRUE WET FLIES

Red October   Cement Overshoe   Titanic

Nymphs

Nymph fishing is comparable to using a Ouija board. You're never quite sure if you're communicating with the Other World or not. The speed at which a trout takes a nymph is roughly comparable to the speed at which the continents are drifting, so you need a finely honed sense of just what a strike feels like.

Nymphing is a kind of fishy Morse Code, and it takes a long time to separate the dots from the dashes. After a while, you will probably be tempted to set the hook every time your rod tip jiggles, which will eventually leave you with a dislocated shoulder and no fish, so be patient. When you've been fishing nymphs for 15 to 20 years, you will learn that the only time you hook trout is when you accidentally bring your rod tip up.

Selecting the Proper Fly...
The Cahill has too much head cement... the Adams has wings that are too long... The Quill Gordon is too bushy..............

Selecting the Proper Fly

Trout are finny Spinozas, possessing incredible intellectual powers far beyond the ken of the average dullard waving a fly rod to and fro. Special tools and minute variations of color and size are needed to entice these Wunderfish into sacrificing themselves. While we dodder about on the hard ground, muttering nonsense about line weights and drag ratios, trout are swimming contentedly, just waiting to make us look even dumber than we already are. Trout fishermen are always paranoid about secret trout plots.

So we dump 600 bucks on a collection of fur and tinsel and bent piano wire, and hope that some freaking fish will have some aesthetic appreciation of how nicely tied the Hendrickson is. Think again.

The names of trout flies are so ludicrous, most fly fishermen are embarrassed to even mention the names of the flies to non-fly fishermen. Some names are calculated for shock effect.

"How was your fishing today?"

"Oh, I tried everything, but the little buggers wouldn't hit anything but a Bitch Creek Nymph."

Bitch Creek Nymph sounds like the title of a soft-core drive-in skin flick, and the fisherman knows it. He's just saying it to sound cool. Other fly names can be tossed off to similar effect:

"Pass me that Rat-Faced McDougall."

Now that sounds appetizing, doesn't it?

But mostly trout fly names are just kind of incomprehensible. The names are usually not at all descriptive, and tend to be fairly cryptic. Who can tell, by the name of the fly itself, just exactly what a Royal Wulff looks like? Or a Badger Bivisible? Or a Quill Gordon?

Some other fly patterns are merely unpronounceable. I have never heard anyone pronounce "Skykomish Sunrise" correctly on the first attempt. The one thing to bear in mind here is this: Flies are basically art, and a trout isn't the Art Critic for *The New York Times*. Trout are able to distinguish dry flies from wet flies, and light flies from dark flies, and large flies from small flies, and that's about the size of it. But you won't be graded on the way the golden pheasant tippets are arranged on your fly.

The History of Fly Fishing

There is quite a body of evidence to suggest that there was primitive fly fishing being practiced in ancient Rome, and by primitive they don't mean that they were using fiberglass rods. Let's put it this way: Trout were probably not very selective. It is said these early fly fishermen dappled long branches out over the stream with very rudimentary—no Swisher-Richards poly dubbing—flies tied on something other than Aeon 3X. It is not known how many fish were caught, although they no doubt would have lied about it had they recorded it.

The next recorded instance is in England, where all proper young men of the 15th century were expected to become expert at fly fishing. They used 18-foot rods, which were probably just heavily limbed willow trees. They also made use of horsehair line, which was free and readily accessible, but today you don't accidentally get kicked in the head if you run down to the store and pick up some Cortland 444. Izaak Walton became the most famous fisherman in England, and for centuries ever after fly fishermen have been using his name as a holy fly-fishing icon. Well, the terrible truth is that Izaak Walton used ... uh ... well, let's clear this up once and for all: He used worms.

No wonder he caught fish. The scene shifted to Scotland, where plaid flies—they're almost impossible to make dubbing for—took the majority of fish in the famous chalk streams.

Gradually, fly fishing spread to the United States where, prior to the advent of fly fishing, all trout were caught with javelins and gill nets. Not too sporting, but effective. Early American fly fishermen stole fly patterns from their English brethren—the British got their revenge by importing the Triumph convertible later in the Industrial Revolution—and proceeded to nearly wipe out the entire species of brook trout in a bit over 100 years. Since there were so few brook trout left, they had to import the brown trout from Germany to keep tackle manufacturers in business.

Then Theodore Gordon burst onto the scene as the author of *The Complete Fly Fisherman*. Gordon was a cranky little fellow who got that way

by tying flies for a living and attempting to make outdoor magazine deadlines. Gordon is revered in America as the father of modern trout angling, and as one of the premier angling writers. Unfortunately, almost all of his journals are now missing; recently, a fragment of one of them turned up:

"I spent eight hours at the fly-tying bench today. I'm about to go cross-eyed. My family thinks I'm certifiable, sitting around and tying little pieces of feather on a hook. I went down to the stream today and got skunked. I busted off 16 Quill Gordons in 45 minutes, and had to come back to tie some more. Tied some up, and went back down to the stream to crack the whip. I slipped on a rock and got pretty wet. I've got to stop fishing in white linen suits. I'm trying to finish the article on the Ten Hot Spots For 1877 for Outdoor Life."

Garden Hackle
tied by Izaak W.

Scottish Chalk Stream Fly

The Compleat Angler, Revised Edition

All manner of thynges have chaynged in the pursuit of and anglinge for Troute. I visited upon an Avon seemingly teeming withe the Trout in question, and was well outfitted with the newest and most advanced Rods, Reels, and Flyes.

Well I knew the Anguished Cryes and consternatione of the angler who equipmente had fayled. I am accustomed to Cane and the symplest of lyne, so I stoode in the Brooke to field teste the new equipment. At once I spyed a risynge Troute and was sore tempted to toss a Garden Hackle or Earthe Worme at the fysh, yet well I recalled the Admonitiones and Warnynge of Purists who do not of necessity neede to catch the Troute. So Goode Sporte that I indeed be, I put asyde the thoughts of the Meat angler and tyed on the most meagre of flyes (size 22 creame midge) and gossamer leader.

Insistently the Troute rose as I importuned him to accept my Tiny insecte. No Luck as Suche, so I tyed on another and another, until I was able to Determine that the Troute in question was a Selective One. One That Won't byte come Helle or Highe Water.

I attempted to execute Rolle Castes and Slyngeshot deliveries of My Forwarde weightede lyne. The Troute rolled and Boiled as if to mocke my Fruitless efforts. More and more pyssed off I became as I maniacally replaced minature terrestrials and teeny nymphes and Gaudy attractors and still the risynge Troute slapped Maerrily on the surface.

I tryed six weights and five weights and even a laughable four weighted rod and lyne and so on. The Troute knew not my Brande Names and Boron Rod and power Butt and engrayved reele, and scarce I coulde place blame on him.

"Screwe you," I mused as a riposte to the Taunts and mockingyne Behaviour of the Troute and I heav'd the Winston rod and the Hardie reele and *The Scientifik angler lyne far into the Brooke. I wente scavenging in the mud for a Large worme and tyed it on to my Olde Cane Pole and tossed it in the Vicinity of the Troute, who tooke it Hooke, lyne and Synkere.*

So I reeled in the God Damned Trout and consumed it on the banke of the Brooke and To Helle with the delicate Presentatione.

A Fly-Fishing Boyhood

I grew up in Minnesota, where the state legislature, consisting of guys who owned gas stations and bait shops selling 9-inch-long sucker minnows, decided to make the state fish the Walleye. A walleye is a kind of highly evolved carp with sharp teeth. Walleyes live in vast schools, and the preferred method of capture is to endlessly drift over them in your 14-foot Deep Vee aluminum boat with an impaled leech and a sinker that could moor the Titanic in high seas. Very sporting.

I fished like this for a couple of years, catching banana-sized walleyes with my dredging unit and wondering if this was all there was to fishing. One day I was cleaning out the garage, and I found my dad's old fly rod, an ancient Shakespeare with a Pflueger Medalist reel and maroon floating line. I took this rig out into the front yard and began flailing around with it, and ultimately became quite expert at making a buggy-whip-like crack, which kept all the animals and small children in the neighborhood at bay. I then discovered my dad's fly box, which was full of huge wet flies, such as the Red Ibis and the notorious Royal Coachman.

I went down to a nearby lake and did my buggy whip impression into the lily pads. Three-inch sunfish immediately fell for my subterfuge, and I discovered the not-inconsiderable joys of not using worms and bobbers to catch these minute fish. I would stand on the shore for hours, catching 40 or 50 sunfish and the occasional bass until my arms got tired. I was not bothered by banana-sized walleyes, which was my way of rebelling against the state legislature's piscatorial imperialism.

Of course, many of my peers in 1974 were experimenting with various strains of marijuana and weighing the pros and cons of Hamm's versus Grain Belt, not the relative merits of the brown trout versus the walleye. I did manage to find a couple of other nerds who were interested in becoming trout fishermen. One of them was considered the Theodore Gordon of Johanna Junior High School because he actually tied his own flies. So I took it up, along with another friend,

who was, unfortunately, color blind and thus turned out chartreuse chenille flies with purple hackle.

Being under driving age, we had to get our mothers to drive us over to Wisconsin to fish in the Kinnikinnick River. The Kinnikinnick is about 30 feet wide and had, at that time, a steady stream of rubber rafters spewing garbage; it's probably been paved over by now and been turned into a subdivision called Troutshire Mews.

The first outing was a complete bust. I put on my dad's bird-hunting vest, and his boots, two sizes too small with a leak in the right foot. I had no idea what I was doing, or how to cast, or what kind of fly to use. I inadvertently got a strike while stripping in excess line. I considered dipping into a secret supply of Uncle Josh's salmon eggs. I went home and daydreamed about leeches and walleyes.

The second time I went, I caught a fish on a fly that I tied myself, which was a Coachman nymph. I noticed that most of my flies came unraveled after about 20 minutes, probably because I was using pink toenail polish as head cement. But I did catch a fat little brown in a long stretch of flat water, and I got so excited I ran back to my friend. He had caught about 15 fish that size. I wondered aloud about whether he was using dynamite.

Still, I thought no more about the walleye, except when I was in a social situation where I then attempted to "pass" as a walleye fisherman: "Ya, I caught about tirty of dem walleyes up on Lake Mille Lacs on a Lindy Rig and so. . . ."

Equipment fever set in quickly. I bought a 3M Phillipson rod for 14 bucks through a mail-order concern called the Fly Fisherman's Bookcase and Tackle Shop. Then I got a red South Bend reel with level-floating line. My next purchase was an unfinished Blackhawk Fenwick graphite rod and new Pflueger Medalist with orange-weight forward line, which was a pretty upscale outfit for the Kinnikinnick River. I felt the trout sensed this and rejected my offering more often based solely on economic principles.

Time passed. I had to give up fly fishing temporarily while I labored in trout-fishing meccas like

Detroit, Michigan, and Columbus, Ohio. I later heard at my high school reunion that my primary trout-fishing buddy was going to Harvard Medical School. It figures that a guy who was good at tying knots and cutting things open would do that. Now he can be paid big money for doing it.

He'll need it to keep up with all the new equipment.

Shopping for Equipment: Fear and Loathing at the Hardware Store

Okay. You've just fallen out of a tree, and you don't know what to buy when you toddle into a fly shop. If you can, go to a small, independent fly shop. Don't go to a hardware store, or this will probably happen:

"Hi, can I help you?"

The salesman's name is Todd. They're all named Todd.

"Yes, I'm interested in buying a fly-fishing outfit. Can you give me a hand?" you say cautiously, seeing the guy's name is Todd.

"Well, I usually work over in Snow Tires, but I think I can get you rigged up. What you need here first is a rod. How about this Aqualinear Mark III, with Genuine Lacquered Line-O-Matic guides, Screw-Loose Reel Seat, and a real bronze cowbell tied to the end?"

"Ah. . . .

"And then you'll need a reel, of course. May I suggest the Rock'N'Reel with Full, Modified, and Improved Choke, Winch-Ratio Gear sprockets, Knurled Plywood CrankMaster handle, and an engraved Art Scene with a Rising Carp in the bullrushes?"

"Ah. . . .

"And then the line, which I think should be this nice 30-pound test lead center SeaDredge Duofilament. You're gonna need it to haul in the big ones."

"Ah. . . .

Then, an interruption on the store PA system: "Todd, pick up line two. Question about Steel-belted radials in Snow Tires. Todd, line two."

Your cue. Make a mad dash for the exit as Todd picks up the phone.

Now go to a real fly shop, but avoid this:

"Hi, I'd like to start fly fishing, and I need some equipment."

"Do you have a reservation?"

"For what?"

"A reservation. To be here. There's also a coat and tie regulation. May we provide one for you?"

"Well . . ."

"We'll squeeze you in. You'll need a rod. This is a Winston cane. Don't touch it. Don't breathe on it. Don't look at it."

"Gee, I. . . .

"How will you be financing this? Citicorp is quoting six points above prime on their Rod Loan Programme. It's sixteen five, without the case. The only reel that fits this particular rod is the Hardy. I told you not to touch it. You're getting vapour on it."

"Ah. . . .

"Eight five, but you'll have to order it today to lock in the interest rate. Our next shipment should be in January '94. They're handmade by trolls and druids in Wales."

Leave. Now.

Marshall McLuhan Angling

With the introduction of home video, and millions of willing cocooning couch potato fly fishermen out there, it was inevitable that more industrious, photogenic fly fishermen would put together trout-fishing trips that can be popped in the old VHS without even having to buy a nonresident license.

There is now a company that sends videotaped trout-fishing trips to your home once a month. You can just sit there with your rod and reel and pretend you're hauling in a big one, even when you're the big one being hauled in.

There are also instructional videos that tell you everything you're doing wrong. Somehow, it is more demeaning to have a Trout-Fishing Legend tell you your double-haul cast was loading wrong than it would be to have your fishing pal do it instead. At least you can tell your pal to mind his own business.

The Trout Fishing Experience

As you begin trout fishing, you will note that you will frequently not catch a fish, or a sucker, or a chub, or even a cold. You will just be standing out in the middle of a river, moving your line around as the trout doze peacefully, oblivious to your machinations and entreaties. There's nothing you can do about it. It happens.

Thanks to the advent of the 1970s and psychobabble, you will find yourself telling yourself all sorts of things in order to justify what seems, at times, like an obscene expense and the seeming inanity of standing out in a stream while all else hibernates. You will need a rationalization, a raison d'être for your lack of trout-catching skills.

We call this The Trout Fishing Experience.

It goes something like this: "Gee, even though I'm not catching fish, and indeed have not caught a fish in the last 72 hours, I'm enjoying this pastoral interlude. It's a time for me to get in touch with nature and all things living, to contemplate my oneness with the biosphere and the cosmos, to muse rhapsodically about my place in the universe whilst I stand in the center of this rushing, raging torrent holding a $400 stick in my hand.

"Note the warbling thrushes, the circling carrion, and the friendly fish and game officer as he grills me relentlessly about my license. It's only a piece of paper, and what is one scrap of parchment in the scheme of it all? I'm out here in the trees, the flowers, the flora and the fauna, the buzzing bees and the kamikaze-esque mosquitoes gnawing gently on my earlobes, communing with God and all his Creation."

At this point you should go home and watch the radio.

Catch and Release: Not a Soviet Plot

Catch and release became popular in the late '60s and early '70s, when there seemed to be a limit on everything but lying politicians. The 1970s were an era of limits; everyone was hung up on preserving the environment. There were cover stories in *Time* and *Newsweek* about the distinct possibility of all life on earth being extinguished by 1979 because of cans and tires floating in rivers, and there was also the growing realization on the part of fishermen that you couldn't catch 212 trout every day and expect to repeat the numbers.

For some, catch and release seemed to be yet another milepost on the short freeway to one-world Communism, where denial of the right to slaughter fish was just another example of big government telling us what to do, where the next exit was the fluoridation of Budweiser.

Who hasn't felt guilty looking at a freezer full of cryogenically preserved rainbows, sitting in their aluminum-foil shrouds never to take a dry fly again?

Trout Recipes

CATCH AND RELEASE! HELLO OUT THERE! CATCH AND RELEASE! READ MY LIPS! CATCH AND RELEASE!

I'm sorry. Thank you.

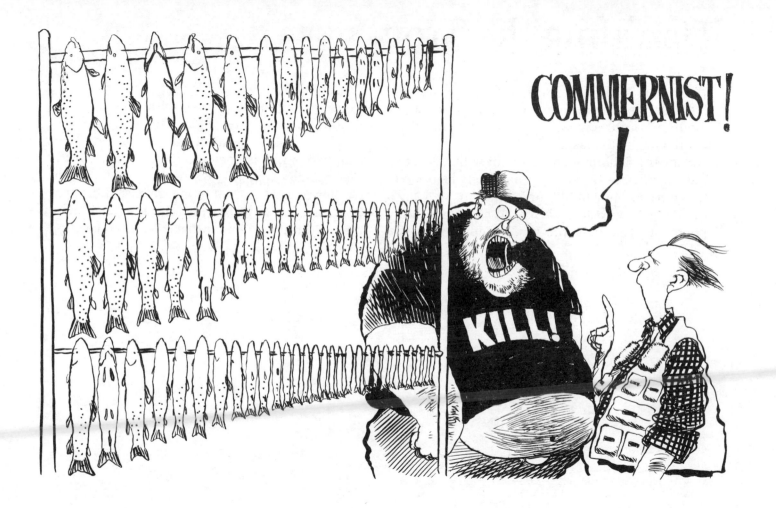

Handling the Trout

Your trout is subdued. He's tired, he's shocked as hell that the juicy little nymph turned out to be a mouthful of fur and wire, and he's looking at the net like it's euthanasia.

Some fly fishermen, not content with just catching a fish, want to examine the trophy before putting it back. They hold it up by the jaw, they lay it on the grass next to their fly rod and have a trout photo op, and they rub their hands all over it, petting it like it was a kitty cat. By this time, the trout is about to say the hell with it and pass out. Feeling sporting, they're going to let him go.

After keeping the trout out of the water for a couple of minutes, they put the trout back in, and then wonder why it looks like the Andrea Doria. Or they return the trout to the water, but they give it a heave-ho, as if it needs a little momentum or they're throwing him for distance, like a javelin.

Dealing with the Fish and Game Officer

Inevitably, you will have a brush with the law as you pursue the wily and elusive trout. The fish and game officer is a lot different from your garden-variety fuzz, in the sense that he seems to have all the time in the world to chat with you and look at your license and make sure your hooks are barbless, inspect your creel, and pat you down for illegal drugs and weapons.

You're probably from the big city. You deal with cops all the time. City cops are in a big hurry, usually, to catch murdering hordes, and dope smugglers from Florida, and jaywalkers, and thus don't take the time to get to know you like a fish and game officer does. He knows this, and is playing off of your expectation that he'll look at your license and then be off to the next pool.

You will be standing in a riffle, and he'll charge in right behind you like a Labrador Retriever, friendly as all hell. You do the citified thing and be cool and distant. Don't do it. He's got a job to do, and he's just after the facts, ma'am, but he'll make a lot of chitchat while you wonder what in Sam Hill he's up to. Be friendly. Smile. Give him your top three fish-producing fly patterns. After he's convinced you don't have 895 dead brown trout in your trunk, he'll probably let you go.

Sometimes they're not so friendly. Well, at first they are, but you're in a heap of trouble if you can't produce your license, boy. In many states, if you don't have your license, the law will just take your gear. All of it. Everything in the car, too, and they'll read you the Riot Act, and you'll feel like a damned idiot. After they've taken your your gear, they send it over to LaCrosse or Butte or Casper or Montpelier, invariably 225 miles from where you live, and auction off your precious Thomas and Thomas for $7.95.

Just a friendly warning from a guy who watched

it happen to a kid who took all his dad's fly fishing equipment out without telling him about it.

It wasn't me, and his dad just about tore his head off.

It really wasn't me. I swear it.

Knots, Intentional and Unintentional

If you've got short, stubby fingers and wear reading glasses, any relaxation you would normally derive from fly fishing is completely eliminated when you try to tie on a fly.

The average trout fly is probably no more than a half-inch long. If you have mediocre close vision, it would be a chore just to find the hook eyelet, let alone pass a piece of monofilament the diameter of a hair—a transparent hair—through it. This is why some older guys give it all up for Ford Fenders and Florescent Day-Glo Cheezmallows.

There are some sociopaths who actually tie their own tapered leaders. When you get to this stage, check yourself into a good mental health facility, because you've gone over the edge. To deliberately tie little microscopic pieces of fishing line together is what Van Gogh would have done if he couldn't have painted.

Currently, leader manufacturers use the "X" system of rating tippet weights. X is a cross, which is a shorthand phrase for cross-eyed, which is what happens when you attempt to tie a fly on a 7X leader. You might as well throw your trout flies out in the middle of the stream for how many strikes you're going to hook with a 7X.

The Differences Between Fly Fishermen and Bait Fishermen

Fly Fishermen	Bait Fishermen
Have names like Roger, Doug, Jon	Have names like Junior, Bubba, Al
Own at least 5 good wool suits	Own at least 5 black T-shirts with beer motif
Volvo, BMW, Jeep Cherokee	'65 Bel Air, '71 LTD, '67 Ford F-250
Floss after brushing	No teeth to speak of
Lawyers, Brokers, Computer Reps	Fix cars
Coronas, Heinekens, St. Pauli Girl	Bud, Bud, Bud
Jog	Smoke Pall Malls
Orvis, Winston, Hardy	Zebco, Eagle Claw, Shakespeare
Talk about fishing experience	Talk about sexual experience
Catch and release	Beat carp to death with baseball bat
Swisher and Richards, Schweibert	Uncle Josh
Matching the hatch	Locally gathered nightcrawlers
Cheese and bread: streamside lunch	Cheese and bread: bait
Fly to Montana to fish	Driving an all-nighter to Northern Wisconsin, stopped for DWI

Yuffies, Hippies, Geezers, and Worm Drowners

NAME: Elliott Abrams Richardson IV
OCCUPATION: Bond Trader
RESIDENCE: Upper East Seventies brownstone, Manhattan
AGE: 35
QUOTE: "Sell."

Elliott makes $730,000 a year trading pieces of paper with French bond traders. It's a stressful life; Elliott used to unwind by taking martinis through an IV bag and inflaming his nasal passages with cocaine, but he decided that he needed a hobby to help him relax. Elliott chose fly fishing because it's a little—not much—cheaper than his recreational drug intake.

Elliott doesn't have a good selection of fly water to indulge his habit, so he usually charters a plane up to Maine or New Hampshire instead of roll casting for condoms—"Chicago Trout" or "Coney Island Whitefish"—in the East River.

This year, Elliott will spend $32,256.50 on fly-fishing equipment. He lives within limousine distance of the Orvis store, and likes to go there on Saturdays with his American Express Platinum/Plutonium card (credit limit: GNP of Australia). To keep a little stress in his hobby, Elliott likes to attempt to tie intricate Scottish salmon flies; this way he can sniff head cement and get a little buzz if his tying technique is a bit off. Elliott caught two browns (aggregate length: 13 inches) and seven brookies (total weight: one lb., two oz.) last year in the Kill rivers. Elliott doesn't like to actually touch fish—"Blows my manicure all to hell"—and thinks he might make a down payment on New Zealand next year so he doesn't have to share any riffles with riffraff.

NAME: Alton "Buzz" Bondo
OCCUPATION: Unemployable
RESIDENCE: Toledo, Ohio, Mobile Villa Garden Estates
AGE: 39 (looks 55)
QUOTE: "Hey, you wanna catch fish, or dontcha? Pass the cheese hooks."

Buzz is a major presence at the U-Ketchum Trout Pond off County Road B. Ohio doesn't have any indigenous trout except for those that live in aquariums, so the U-Ketchum is a big attraction for the fly-fishing impaired.

Buzz is usually relaxed—okay, anesthetized—so he doesn't really fish for the pure relaxation of it all. It's just another way to get away from his wife (Babs, Beauty Consultant, Miss Maumee River Third Place runner-up, 1966), and kids (Alton Jr., 17, Du Wayne, 16, Wayne Lee, 15, Earl, 13, Shirl, 12, and Bobbie Lou, 11).

Buzz ties fly patterns of his own creation: The Cheez Whiz, Velveeta Special, Kraft's Hopper, Doughball Coachman, Corn Doctor, Maize Quill, Gold-Ribbed Onion Mallow, and the old reliable Night's Crawler.

Buzz caught 320 trout last year at 50 cents a whack, which is about 800 times cheaper than Elliott's per-fish cost ratio.

NAME: Orvis Bodmer Thomas
OCCUPATION: Geezer
RESIDENCE: Hidden Valley Ranch, Antelope, Oregon (formerly Rajneesh, Oregon)
AGE: 77 ("Hell, I can remember when Christ was a corporal.")
QUOTE: "Get the hell outta my drift, you yuppie son of a bitch, or I'll put a crease in your noodle."

Orv has been fishing the same stretch of the Deschutes for 45 years, and doesn't like it when the investment bankers and lawyers from Portland and Seattle come down in their Blazers and Eddie Bauer Broncos and splash into the river and jangle up the dry-fly water with lousy casts. "A guy gets a subscription to *Fly Fisherman*, and all of a sudden he's in my hole slinging around the wrong patterns and leaving white wine bottles all over the goddam bank."

Orv doesn't go in for fancy equipment, either. "I gotta Shakespeare glass Wonderod and a Pflueger Medalist I bought in 1951, and the fish don't seem to give a squat."

Orv on streamside etiquette: "I'll streamside etiquette you, mister. Now get the hell outta here before I go back to the house and get my Browning Over and Under."

Orv on his fly patterns: "I wouldn't tell you my patterns for all the tea in China, buster, so why don't you hightail it back to Seattle and put your yellow tie back on."

NAME: Ralph Waldo Walden
OCCUPATION: Prose poet, ectopian
RESIDENCE: "I don't believe in property."
AGE: 44 ("What did I do during the '60s? Hey . . .
I was the '60s.")
QUOTE: "Communing with trout is almost as
good as two tabs of Purple Microdot."

Ralph is a strong advocate of The Trout Fishing
Experience. Shedding the shackles of society and
just being there with the trout—catching is op-
tional—is the object of the game. Heck, you don't
even need a rod.

Ralph makes his own rods—"There's no better
rod material than Mother Nature, dude." What-
ever happens to be available at streamside is fair
game; sometimes it's a willow switch, and other
times it's a 25-foot tree branch. Lousy feel, but a
hell of a backcast. Ralph won't tie any pattern that
requires using material that has been killed by
man, which leaves him with pink chenille and
tinsel. Ralph doesn't catch a lot of fish.

But it's not the fish; it's being out there, rapping
with the browns and the brookies and getting
good vibes from the stream and the insects and
nature.

And the Purple Microdot.

NAME: Kid
OCCUPATION: Third-grade student
RESIDENCE: Mom and Dad's house
AGE: 8. And a half.
QUOTE: "I was just sitting there with my Snoopy reel when this big fish bit my hook."

There is the kid you always see on the stream. You're all decked out in your trout-capturing togs and this kid is sitting over a cutbank with his feet in the water, holding a four-foot rod with the closed face reel. You walk up to the kid, very patronizing, and smile beatifically down on this precious tot. "Any luck?" you ask in your child-addressing voice.

"Just this," the kid says, pointing to a 24-inch brown sticking halfway out of a Day-Glo orange sand bucket. The kid adds, as you pick up your bricks, that he caught it on Hula-popper with a muskie-sized bobber. You have been floating a size-20 sulphur emerger over the cutbank for about three hours before the kid shows up, and suddenly, you're offering the kid 20 bucks and your lunch for the rig. He declines.

NAME: Watson Crick
OCCUPATION: Systems analyst
RESIDENCE: Condo, Silicon Valley
AGE: Median
QUOTE: "All fishing systems nominal"

Watson can't have fun fly fishing unless he's got all the latest high-tech breakthrough equipment. He knows the density of his boron rod, the tensile strength of his 400-grain line, the drag coefficient of his fly, how much wind resistance a parachute wing Adams has versus a hackle wing, the porosity of elk hair, the exact chemical composition of Gehrke's Gink, the gear ratio on his multiplier, the genus and species of every single aquatic insect, the solunar tables, the viscosity of the water's meniscus, the diameter of his leader in thousandths of an inch, the insulative qualities of his waders, the relative merits of weight-forward line in relation to double taper, the aerodynamic qualities of the Muddler Minnow, the effect of atmospheric pressure on the trout's lateral line, and the toll-free phone numbers of all his tackle manufacturers.

But he doesn't catch any fish.

Lists

FIVE WORST TROUT FISHING AREAS

1. Ohio

2. The moon

3. Your bathtub

4. Greenwich Village

5. Love Canal

FIVE WORST WAYS TO ASK FOR FISHING INFORMATION IN A LOCAL FLY FISHING SHOP

1. "What do you hicks use to catch rainbows around these parts?"

2. "Excuse me, but you smell like you know where the fish might be."

3. "Me from Big City Back East. New York! Want to catch fish. Rainbows! You 'um know where?"

4. "I'll give you all rides in my new Bronco if you tell me where the fish are!"

5. You won't get to Number 5.

THE LARGEST TROUT EVER CAUGHT

1. Rainbow trout record—42 lbs. 2 oz

2. Brook trout record—14 lbs. 8 oz

3. Brown trout record—35 lbs. 15 oz

4. Cutthroat trout record—41 lbs

5. Golden trout record—11 lbs

TEN PHRASES TO NEVER USE IN THE PRESENCE OF A FLY FISHERMAN

1. Bobber

2. Pork Rind

3. Plastic worms

4. Mister Twister

5. Rapala

6. Worm syringe

7. Spanish Fly Fish Ointment

8. Chumming

9. Bass Tracker

10. Ford Fender

FIVE WEIRDEST FLY NAMES

1. Mormon Girl
2. Bumblepuppy
3. Rat-Faced McDougall
4. Female Beaverkill
5. Parmacheene Belle

FIVE NICKNAMES TO AVOID CALLING YOUR FRIENDS IN DAN BAILEY'S FLY SHOP

1. Chaps
2. Old Sport
3. Good Fellow
4. Mon Chéri
5. Sailor

TWO PRESIDENTS WHO WERE AVID FLY FISHERMEN

1. Jimmy Carter

2. Warren G. Harding

3. This says something, but I don't know what.

FIVE MOST COMMON VEHICLES SEEN AT TROUT FISHING STREAMS, 1965

1. International Harvester Scout

2. Jeep

3. Ford Pickup

4. GMC Pickup

4. Dodge Pickup

FIVE MOST COMMON VEHICLES SEEN AT TROUT-FISHING STREAM, PRESENT DAY

1. Volvo station wagon with baby car seat

2. BMW

3. Mercedes-Benz

4. Porsche

5. Jeep Cherokee

Fishionary

ACTION—What you don't get after fishing all day with your new $700 fly-fishing outfit.

ATTRACTOR FLY—A fly that attracts so much attention that it scares the bejesus out of the trout.

BACKING—As in Financial backing, which is what you need to begin fly fishing.

BANK—Where you go to get financial backing to begin fly fishing.

BAR—Where you go after you have busted off 31 flies in two hours.

BARB—A woman you dated in college that you were thinking about when you missed the umpteenth strike of the day.

BASS—Trash fish sought by guys in floating Pontiac Firebirds.

BASSHOLES—Guys who fish for bass.

CAST—What you wear on your leg or arm after you've fallen on the slimy boulders at the bottom of the stream.

CATCH AND RELEASE—What game wardens do to you when you have 61 fish in your cooler and the limit is 5.

CREEL—An empty wicker basket.

CUTTHROAT TROUT—Aren't they all?

DEER HAIR—Fly-tying material available from deer barber.

DENSITY—The average intelligence level of a bait fisherman.

DRAG—How they look for drowned fishermen.

DRAG-FREE DRIFT—A stream where there are no transvestites present.

DREDGING—See Trolling.

DRESS—What the transvestites wear at streamside.

DRY FLY—Theoretical concept not yet perfected, like the Strategic Defense Initiative.

EMERGER—A fly fisherman after a fall.

FINGERLING—A fully grown brook trout.

FLOTANT—Lead in a liquid state.

FLY—An inaccessible vent in your trousers covered up by several layers of clothing and chest waders that you can't get to in time.

FLY TYING—Number one hobby in mental health facilities.

HACKLE—More expensive than sable per square inch.

HOOK—Sales pitch expression used in conjunction with the words "line" and "sinker" by high-priced fly-fishing outfitters after selling a piece of graphite for $500.

KNOTLESS—State of fly-fishing nirvana.

LEADER—Length of monofilament used to ease breaking off of fly by trout.

LEECH—Friend who borrows flies and never buys any of his own.

LINE—Exaggerated number of fish caught when relating fishing trip to friends, as in "giving them a line."

MANIPULATE—Purpose of fly-fishing advertising.

MINNOW— See Fingerling.

NET—What you're ready for after you've tied flies.

PICKUP—Made scramble to retrieve flies after fly box is turned over accidentally in stream.

POCKET WATER—The level to which the water reaches when you step in a hole while wearing your hip boots.

POLTERGEIST—See Trout.

POUND TEST—The amount of effort you have to put into deliberately busting off a fly.

PRESENTATION—Formerly known as a good cast.

PUMPING THE TROUT—A fly fisherman's only exercise.

PUT AND TAKE—Destroying the village in order to save it.

READING WATER—Place to haul out your book when the fish aren't biting.

REEL—What you do when you see how much a Hardy costs.

RISING FISH—Optical illusion, like an oasis.

SCHOOL—As in Master's degree in Entomology, which you may feel that you need after a couple of fishless trips.

SELECTIVE—Not hungry.

SPINNING—The only acceptable one is the way Gandhi did it.

SPOOK—Something that happens to trout the second you get in the water.

STEELHEAD—Great white whale.

STRIPPING—Too obvious a joke.

STUDS—Another one that's too obvious.

TAILWATER—Water that you slip and land on your tail in.

TAPER—A broken rod that has been repaired with duct tape.

TERRESTRIAL INSECT—An oxymoron, since there is no such thing as an extraterrestrial insect.

TREBLE HOOK—Hook that sends out high-frequency sounds.

TROLLING—See *Dredging*.

TROUT—See *Poltergeist*.

TWITCH—A nervous disorder brought on by excessive fly tying or leader tying.

WATER—Where trout hang out.

ABOUT THE AUTHOR

Jack Ohman is the editorial cartoonist for *The Oregonian*. His work is syndicated in 175 newspapers in the U.S. and overseas. He goes fly fishing less often than he would like.